The Leadership Event:

The Moments of True Leadership that Move Organizations

2nd Edition, Revised
September 2006

Warren Blank
Aaron Brown

D0873460

The Leadership Event
ISBN No. _____

Copyright © 2004, 2006 by Warren Blank and Aaron Brown.
2nd Edition, Revised
All rights reserved. Printed in the United States of America.

Published by: The Leadership Group Press

Printing
10 9 8 7 6 5 4 3 2

9. Registration Number: TXu-1-221-689
Title: The leadership event: the moments of true leadership that move organizations.
Description: 59 p.
Claimant: acWarren Blank, 1948-, & acAaron Brown, 1950-
Created: 2004

Registered: 5Jul05

Special Codes: 1/B

For Ray W. Alvord

— A leader who created many moments that made a positive difference, a great mentor, and a life-long friend. Thanks.

Warren

For Sharon S. Senecal

— A friend, a peer, a boss, and a trusted colleague who provided leadership opportunities when others were afraid! Thanks.

Aaron

Acknowledgments

We are deeply indebted to many people who demonstrated great leadership in so many moments and who set a standard of excellence to develop leadership around them.

Specifically, we want to recognize Tom Donaldson, Wayne Foster, Conniesue Oldham, Rob Kramer, Jim Mayer, Rossie Carnes, and Linda Winner.

We also want to thank Carrolle Rushford, Lani Duarte Robbins, and Joe and Nancy Mangino for their very valuable support, critique, and energy in helping us write this manuscript.

We also want to thank the 2,000 + readers of the first edition. We hope you found it "eventful"!

Contents

The Leadership Event

Have you ever been in a meeting and suggested a way to solve a problem and the entire group willingly agreed with you and was motivated to carry out your course of action?

Can you recall a time when a team member proposed an action that you thought would be very useful so you spoke up to support it? As a result, the entire team joined in and adopted the path of action.

Your experience illustrates the Leadership Event.

Leadership Events are the critical moments that move organizations. Like bursts of energy, they ignite people to move into action. Leadership Events drive groups, organizations, societies, and nations towards positive outcomes.

Leadership Events create the force necessary to overcome obstacles and exploit possibilities. They fill in the "white space" or voids when the established rules, policies, and procedures do not apply or are an obstacle to move towards a desired goal.

Leadership Events define the core reality of "true leadership" which we define as an interaction, a committed relationship, between the leader and followers.

Leadership Events, like any event in nature, have a beginning, a middle, and an end. The beginning of the Leadership Event occurs when someone (the "leader") offers a direction. The event's "middle" is the meaningful moment that happens when one or many others (the "followers") willingly support the direction.

No one can be a "true leader" without unforced or willing followers. Followers emerge only in response to a leader's course of action. The Leadership Event ends upon accomplishment of the leader's action or when another direction is suggested.

Anyone can contribute to the meaningful moments called Leadership Events. You do not have to be the boss or "in charge" to be a "true leader," and create leadership events.

Our best bosses were, of course, ones we wanted to follow. Anyone, including the boss, can "take the lead" and offer direction. Anyone can be a willing "first follower," the person who steps up first and whose commitment creates the necessary momentum to fulfill the leader's direction. Such a contribution takes both courage and skill.

Leadership Events occur up and down the corporate and governmental ladder. It is the multiple Leadership Events that occur daily at all levels that enable people and organizations to succeed over the long term in any endeavor. Success in any group action depends on more and better "true leadership" enacted by more people taking part in Leadership Events.

Key Factors

There are six key factors necessary to create true leadership. You must:

✔ Understand the dynamics of the Leadership Event

✔ Create Leadership Events

✔ Establish the necessary ground work by building and sustaining credible relationships

✔ Reinforce Leadership Events when they occur

✔ Block Negative Leadership Events that do not serve an organization's real purpose

✔ Develop and apply an action plan to become more skillful in creating Leadership Events

The Critical Question

Are you willing to commit to implement the six key areas on a regular and consistent basis as part of an on-going self-development effort?

Your answer to this critical question underlies all other considerations because leadership skills are not in-born. It is true that some people are born with preferences and tendencies that enable them to develop leadership skills more easily in the same way some people are born with physical attributes that support more gifted athletic efforts. For example, the great basketball player Shaquille (Shaq) O'Neal stands over seven feet tall and weighs over 330 pounds placing him head and shoulders above others on the basketball court. Shaq can attack the basket more easily because of his size.

And some people are born with opportunities and role models that make it easier to build up leadership competence. Imagine being born into the Kennedy, Bush, or Ghandi families and wanting to go into politics. Envision having Bill Gates, Warren Buffett, or Henry Ford as your father and seeking a career in business. Think about growing up in the Martin Luther King, Jr., Gloria Steinman, or Caesar Chavez family with a desire to be a social justice activist. Such fortuitous development, surrounded by people who created major Leadership Events throughout their lives, could only increase the possibilities to learn and apply the necessary skills to create positive leadership events.

Yet, even those born with the potential or "gifts" related to leadership skill could not master those latent talents without a high level of personal desire, motive, will, or intent. Being born into a specific family does not assure skill development. To master any complex task, people must want to emulate the models available.

Besides, at this point it does not matter what you were born with or the role models you had while growing up. What matters now is what you do with your capacities. Think of the many athletes who had incredible "natural gifts" of speed, strength, and endurance yet failed to make it to the professional ranks or never lived up to their potential as a pro because they lacked commitment and the requisite work ethic to build on their "natural" advantages.

True Leadership Begins With the "W Factor"

To manifest true leadership and create Leadership Events requires you first get clear about the "W Factor" — your personal *Will* or motivation.

Leadership Events occur based on a person's desire to offer a course of action and/or a willingness to voluntarily support the path. The will to step up in the face of uncertainty as the leader or first follower precedes all else.

The "W Factor," which exists inside each of us, reflects our sense of "Self" — our assumptions, beliefs, values and our quality of awareness, or consciousness, about who we are and what we want to become.

No amount of pay or barter for perks can create or sustain the motivation to step up as a leader or first follower. The challenge and risks are too high.

You could take the lead and have your idea criticized as foolish or unrealistic. Your boss could be threatened by your initiative and negate your influence by commanding other subordinates not to accept it. A jealous coworker could sabotage your initiative by spreading false information or stab you in the back because of their own passion for power.

Even if you initially gain followers, they can always flee in favor of someone else. Follower support can be fickle. If some followers support you long enough to carry out your direction, others who control critical resources might withhold them and thwart your capacity to complete your plan. And, your direction might be fully carried out and then turn out to be wrong which could crush your credibility.

There are no guarantees in the leadership arena because taking the lead is fraught with risk and uncertainty.

First followers also face risk. You may be the only one who supports another's direction and then have to stand alone and vulnerable because no one else is willing to stand behind an idea. Peers and coworkers might align against you and deride your support if they do not agree with the leader's course. Your "boss" may not agree with an initiative and perceive your support of it in a negative way.

And, assume your first followership does generate enough energy so that others do follow. If the course of action turns out to be ineffective or an outright failure, you will be blamed since, "You were the one who got everyone else to buy in to 'that idea.'"

To create Leadership Events requires getting clear on the "W Factor" and making a decision that true leadership begins as an inside job. Your motivation to take true leadership initiative stems from an internal commitment to serve customers, achieve valued goals, and fulfill the organization's mission and vision.

You have to believe, based on how you perceive yourself, that it is worth it to lead or to be the first follower.

Your efforts may gain recognition, status, and accolades within an organization and in the eyes of others. More pay or other perks might be offered. But these rewards cannot sustain you in the long run since they are external. In your quiet moments, when you are with only your "self," the inner sense of "I" we all possess, the reward has to come from within.

The moment of victory is too short to make it the only thing worth playing for. Take the necessary time to get in touch with the structure of your "W Factor."

Assess Your "W Factor" Ask yourself the following essential questions:

- ✔ Do you want to take the necessary initiative to be part of the true leadership in your organization and contribute to creating Leadership Events?

- ✔ Will you commit to creating Leadership Events that support your organization's primary purpose (vision, mission, and values) and serve its customers (both external and internal)?

- ✔ Is your sense of "self" strong enough to consistently recognize and reinforce others who manifest Leadership Events?

- ✔ Can you summon the courage to diplomatically counter instances when others take action that does not serve an organization's vision, mission, and values?

✔ Will you work continuously on your own development through a formal action plan to improve your true leadership skills?

We assume your answers to these questions are an emphatic "Yes!" — which is why you are reading these words and perhaps sharing them with others. We congratulate you for your initiative, strength, commitment, courage, and action orientation.

Now you need to begin your personal journey to become more skillful at doing what it takes to create Leadership Events. Let's start by describing the mechanics of the Leadership Event.

The Dynamics of the Leadership Event

The Leadership Event occurs as an intersection of its three key components (see below) which always occur in a context defined by the larger environment. The components are:

- ✔ Leader
- ✔ First Follower
- ✔ Situation

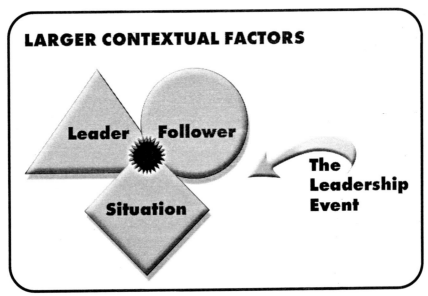

Components of the Leadership Event

The Leader Role

The leader provides direction. The direction could be as grand as a vision which defines an organization's realistic, credible, and attractive future. Or the leader's direction could be a simple idea on how to serve a specific customer or minimize the negative impact of a current process.

Taking the lead — offering direction — represents the starting point of the Leadership Event. Without the leader's willingness to step up and take the risk of initiative to offer a course of action, leadership does not occur.

The leader could be a manager, a person "in charge." Managers have formal authority and can also demand that subordinates comply with their directives. Managers become leaders when they gain willing followers not when they coerce or dominate staff based on their position of power.

A subordinate can be a leader by gaining the support of his/her manager. Think of your best bosses. Did they frequently follow you when you offered a course of action? Were they willing to support your ideas even though they were "in charge?"

The leader could also be a co-worker, peer, partner, customer, supplier, or contractor who does not work for the organization. True leaders chart a course of action and gain the voluntary commitment of others.

That means followers matter. They are the other side of the leadership coin. Offering direction, even if it is noble and needed, and not gaining support, is simply making conversation.

The First Follower Role

The first follower supports the leader's direction first. The first follower speaks up and agrees with the leader's course of action or steps up and clarifies why the leader's direction will serve the group or organization.

The first follower's support creates the necessary momentum to catalyze a group, organization, society, or nation into action in support of the leader. Without the overt support from a first follower, the leader's direction falls flat.

Think of your own experience. Have there been times when you offered an idea and no one spoke up to champion your direction? Your initiative died on the table. Perhaps after the meeting someone remarked to you, "That was a good idea." Yet, they did not speak up when it counted, so your direction had no impact and apparently fell on deaf ears.

The first follower's support is as essential to the Leadership Event as the leader's initiative.

True leadership occurs only when first followers take the risk to support the leader. The first follower's initial commitment may inspire enough others to join the leader's course. In such cases, the leader and first follower gain enough additional acceptance for the direction to be adopted by the group or organization.

First followers could be managers, subordinates, co-workers, company peers, customers, suppliers, contractors or partners from outside the organization.

Again, consider your own experience. Have you at times willingly followed your boss, which means backed her or him, because you believed in the course of action? Recall times when you stood up in favor of a peer, coworker, or even subordinate in response to a path that you felt was worthy.

Sometimes you only need one first follower to move an organization. Consider an idea you think will support the organization's vision, mission, and values and serve all its customers. Could that initiative become wide-spread if you could get the head of your organization to be your first follower?

Imagine you get the willing support or your organization's most senior person. Two things can then happen. Others may also support the idea since they trust and rely on the big boss to give direction. Or, the big boss could require others to comply with the direction because of her/his formal authority.

Management power stems from the right to demand, command and require. True leadership power instills desire, inspires, and creates commitment. When the "big boss" (Chairman, CEO, President, Agency Secretary or

Administrator) becomes your first follower, you become the true leader. The big boss could then require others to carry out your direction by using her/his formal authority. Or, the big boss could become a true leader and inspire others to want to follow. When the big boss gets others to carry out your initiative, he/she aligns the organization toward your leadership direction.

First followers have to consider the impact their alliance creates. Their support actually transforms a person into "the leader" which can create two potential challenges.

Followers have to live with the leader's direction and do the necessary work to carry it out. Followers can always turn and run, but that can create problems of trust and loyalty between them and others.

Followers may also have to comply with those whom they willingly support if, by willingly following, the person obtains the formal authority of position power.

This is what happens when people vote in a democracy for any office. The public gives formal power to the President, a Congressperson, or City Council member by virtue of their vote. Politicians then have the right to "govern" the people. They then have institutional authority to take action for their term of office. Followers give them that power and must obey it.

A similar result occurs when an organization hires a person to be a manager whether it be CEO or first line supervisor. Once hired and given managerial or position power, the person can dictate and require subordinates do what they are told.

In both politics and business, people can get stuck with bad choices. Think about the political scandals over the last 40 years. Recall the savings and loan scams of the 1980s. Remember the accounting rules violations and devious business practices of the 1990s and early 2000s.

In a democracy we can rectify bad choices by voting for someone else. But, while a person is in office, the public has to live with their "leaders" for their term. In organizations, changing the guard can be tougher since managers typically do not have a "term" of office. First followers must always consider the impact their support creates.

The Situation

Leaders and followers always operate in a context. The situation defines the multitude of variables that impact when and how leaders lead and followers follow. For example, consider a complex situation with many long-term uncertainties such as transforming a large, bureaucratic organization into a less "stove-piped," more customer focused, and team based entity.

The leader's initial direction could be just broad outlines of what could be done to begin to address those uncertainties.

Other situations could call for more fully thought out and detailed plans of action. Take a situation involving a single customer or specific aspect of product or service quality. The leader's direction could focus only on this one customer or only a narrow aspect of the customer's needs. Or, the leader's direction could be a laser-like idea about the specific quality issue.

The situation could require involving many other parties so that multiple constituents are served. The situation might demand an immediate course of engagement to urgent and important but short-term problems.

Situations can also demand direction that involves the expansion, extension, or increase of activity, or they can be best benefitted by courses of action that contract, limit, and decrease what a group or organization does.

Followers respond to the leader's direction in precise concert with their perception of situational realities.

In each of the situational illustrations in the previous paragraph, followers calculate the leader's direction in terms of how the followers interpret the situation. For example, followers support either a broadly outlined or narrowly focused directive when they agree that the situation calls for such actions.

Leaders and followers achieve desired results based on how they monitor the environment and in terms of how they compare and contrast alternatives.

Critical Characteristics

L eadership Events have important qualities based on how many people they involve and the extent to which they have impact over time.

Leadership Events Can Be Broad or Localized

Some Leadership Events are "broad" which means many people support a leader's initiative. Recall Reverend Martin Luther King's "I Have A Dream" speech at the Lincoln Memorial in 1963. An estimated one million people watched and listened to Dr. King's stirring vision of freedom and justice for all Americans. The main message King communicated still inspires many people today.

Think of a company executive at an all-hands meeting who offers a plan that motivates the entire staff to want to follow.

Broad Leadership Events make headlines and become the stuff of books and movies. They are the exception however. Most leadership occurs in more localized settings. A leader galvanizes a small group in a meeting. A leader arouses the energy of a work team. Or, a leader generates the commitment of just one other person.

Localized Leadership Events are more frequent since people spend most of their time in circumstances involving a group, team, or single individuals. Think of your work career. How many all-hands meetings do you attend each year? How often are you in a large crowd? Furthermore, the chances of gaining followers is usually greater in a smaller group than in a large group setting.

Leadership Events Can Be Brief or Enduring

The majority of Leadership Events occur as brief connections between leaders and followers. For example, someone suggests a solution to resolve a customer problem during a meeting. Another person supports the idea. A moment of true leadership occurs to move the group forward.

Then another person offers a way to implement the solution in a timely and cost effective way. Several meeting members chime in with enthusiastic agreement which defines another moment of true leadership. A third person then clarifies how to get the necessary resources to carry out the other two actions. Agreement comes from everyone about that path. And one more moment of true leadership moves the participants to achieve desired results.

Some Leadership Events have an enduring quality. For example, Margaret Thatcher maintained a core of willing followers throughout her 12 year tenure as Great Britain's Prime Minister. Jack Welch maintained the support of many at General Electric for twenty years. Franklin Roosevelt won an unprecedented four Presidential elections.

Enduring Leadership Events illustrate two realities about leaders and followers. First, some leaders step up on a regular and continuous basis and offer courses of action that consistently gain willing followers. Ghandi beat the drum for a free India for 40 years. Sam Walton guided Wal-Mart for over 20 years. Alice Paul championed the cause for women's rights in America from 1913 until her death in 1977.

Such individuals are the well known and highly admired "big" leaders. They deserve the leader label.

A second reality of enduring Leadership Events is that some followers commit to certain people with unwavering, unquestioning loyalty. Team members work tirelessly for a person they believe in. Junior military officers tell their captain they will "Go down with the ship," because they have pledged themselves to the person. Voters remain loyal to "their candidate" even though reporters reveal previously unknown negative information.

Yet most Leadership Events have a short shelf-life. This is the tenuous reality of leadership. People can lose interest in a leader's particular path or no longer feel the leader's direction meets their needs. Consider how George H.W. Bush could not get 37% of the vote in the 1992 Presidential election despite the fact that he had a 90% approval rating only 18 months earlier.

In the early 1990s, General Motors' Board of Directors deposed Robert Stempel because they felt he could not steer the firm onto the right track even though he had a 30 year career of positive impact on the company.

Gaining willing followers on a regular basis to create enduring Leadership Events requires capturing and recapturing followers' commitment. Followers may interpret situations in ways vastly different from those who want to lead. Dramatic changes in circumstance can stymie some so they cannot come up with courses of action that attract followers.

Most Leadership Events occur as a series of leader-follower interactions. Just as a motion picture is made up of many separate frames, the sequence of Leadership Events may appear as continuous because some leaders manifest multiple leadership events by repeatedly gaining followers over time.

Most leaders can step up in localized settings and gain sets of followers. This is where most successful organizations gain their momentum. Multiple, localized Leadership Events move small group meetings forward, inspire a few individuals to action, or define direction for one person.

Create Leadership Events

Both leaders and first followers participate as co-contributors to the moments that move organizations. While they provide different elements, the Leadership Events occur as a unified whole of those elements. Like a dance between two well matched partners — picture Fred Astaire and Ginger Rogers moving together gracefully across the floor — the Leadership Event's power and impact comes when both leaders and followers:

✔ Monitor and Assess the Situation
   Read situations on a regular and consistent basis to determine which courses of action best meet the challenges of the circumstance you face

✔ Take the Initiative
   Lead by gaining willing followers to support a direction suitable to the situation and be "first follower ready" by offering support to others whose direction you perceive as appropriate for the situation and will support the organization's purpose.

Monitor and Assess the Situation

Leadership Events always occur in a context. There is no value in offering a direction that does not match some need or possibility. No one will follow a leader's course of action that does not accurately reflect some aspect of the situation.

Leaders and first followers must monitor and assess or "read" the situation as precisely as possible. They need to recognize what is going on and then decide how to respond in ways appropriate to situational demands and options.

It is the leader and first follower's capacity to perceive, interpret, and respond to situations that determines the course of action they provide or support.

Ask three important questions to effectively read the situation:

- ✔ What must be monitored and assessed?

- ✔ When does the situation have to be monitored and assessed?

- ✔ How do the leader and first followers actually "read" the situation so they know what to do?

The ideal answers are:

✔ Everything

✔ All the time

✔ In any way possible...

Ideal...but not very practical. A more reasonable approach is to continuously move towards the ideal by seeking a percentage of perfection.

To do this, consider first what you could monitor and assess. Recognize that, in the ideal, leadership is a response that:

✔ Addresses problems and identifies opportunities—both the big picture and the local level of group-individual activity

✔ Occurs as part of a structured routine and reflects spontaneous readiness

✔ Deals with task issues, what the group or organization must do, attends to process issues, and how the group or organization operates

It may not be possible to read all these factors. It is possible to spend some time on each.

Monitor the Big Picture: Give overt attention regarding obstacles and possibilities in areas such as:

- ✔ Overall competitive environment: What are other important players in your market or agency environment doing (e.g., regarding product development or differentiation, customer service, expansion into new areas, etc.)?

- ✔ Technological advances: What new developments could impact your business or core organizational functions?

- ✔ Social-political factors: What trends seem to be emerging that affect the organization?

- ✔ Organizational "purpose" factors: How does the current vision, mission and values match external and internal capacities?

- ✔ Corporate wide functions: What is happening within the policy, finance, production, marketing, and human resources areas?

✔ Organizational-wide processes: What impact do current systems (e.g., decision making, communication, performance management, succession planning, recruitment, selection, orientation, and training, etc.) have on the total enterprise? And what organizational changes are on the horizon such as a new senior executive coming on board with a new approach to managing the organization?

Assess the Local Level of Groups and Individuals: Focus on problems and possibilities at more local levels by purposefully attending to issues related to:

✔ Specific customers and suppliers especially those who provide the most value to organizational success: What are their needs, wants, and interests?

✔ Individual product or service quality factors: What is important about how they are being created, refined, and received?

✔ Unit or small group functions: What is happening at the local level in the policy, finance, production, marketing, and human resources areas?

✔ Specific goals or milestones: How well do they translate into necessary steps for success given local level realities?

✔ Group and individual processes: What outcomes result based on how people interact at meetings including how they make specific decisions, communicate, support others, deal with conflict, etc.?

To effectively consider any of these areas requires that you deal with the "When" aspect of monitoring the situation.

Again, the ideal would be to monitor all the time. Move towards the ideal by using already established structured activities and by being spontaneous when you monitor.

Establish Structured Times to Monitor: You already know that some situations require heightened focus on the need to create true leadership. Successful situational assessment requires setting your mind to monitor during these times. Formal and informal interactions are the front-line where leadership needs to occur since that is where people typically consider problems and possibilities. Ratchet up your attention power when people get together and discuss problems and possibilities.

Keep a close eye on task and process challenges during regularly scheduled "formal" meetings. Such meetings typically have an established purpose. Compare the meeting's purpose with the *"What"* aspect of questions to monitor.

Watch for signals that indicate stumbling blocks and signs that suggest ways to solve problems. Listen for openings that offer opportunities.

Monitoring and assessing also needs to be part of your time away from others. Schedule a "meeting with yourself" to use specific times alone in a proactive manner to survey information related to your position requirements.

Seek information and insights that suggest a gap between what is and what could be if someone (YOU) would take the lead.

Set your mind to focus on analyzing situations even for a few minutes a day during your travel time to work. Consider and calculate anything that impacts current effectiveness or could be important in the near and longer-term future.

Creating time to just think about the *"What"* issues can provide clues and insights into potential obstacles and opportunities that need leadership direction.

Attend annual professional association conferences relevant to your industry or profession to monitor what other organizations are doing or to learn about new research results.

Develop Unstructured Times to Monitor: Informal interactions define important times to spontaneously move into a monitor and assess mode of situational factors. Being "spontaneously ready" during unstructured times allows you to recognize when something pops up during an encounter in the hallway, in an unplanned gathering of several people around the "water cooler," or during an unexpected call from a colleague.

Recognize that such interactions represent "clues" or "signals" about possible problems and possibilities related to the task and process issues that requires leadership direction. Instead of dismissing the information, turn on your situational awareness to more fully understand the issue, identify root causes, and consider alternate actions.

How you monitor and assess determines the type of information you get and the courses of action you create. We defined the ideal as "in any way possible." Approach the ideal by using methods that add value, reveal patterns, uncover assumptions, suggest scenarios, and rely on varied approaches.

Monitor for Added Value: Talking and listening to others, reading, and thinking on your own in structured and spontaneous ways bring new information and insights. They may not necessarily suggest leadership direction or provide clarity about underlying root causes. And they might.

Leadership action needs to add something of value so that people want to follow it and remain committed to its course. It must make a meaningful difference.

Situational awareness needs to go deep to uncover the need to lead and reveal sources of action that add value.

Listen for the "values messages" that define what is good or bad, right or wrong, important or unimportant.

Values determine how people evaluate what they want to accomplish and which means they use to accomplish particular ends. An organization's values reflect its collective sense of what is highly regarded, frowned upon, or considered impermissible.

Value messages get communicated in conversations all the time. Statements such as, "Management lied to us" and "We can't trust this organization," can signal a potentially volatile situation regarding an organization's culture. Comments such as, "Customers can be a pain," could reveal serious flaws in people's understanding of their role.

Questions like, "Can we do that?" can imply a lack of empowerment among staff or an overly rule-minded management system. Positive values messages such as, "We want to make a difference in this area," and, "We need to go after this opening quickly," can also signal something in a situation that deserves leadership action.

Monitor Patterns: Seek the "pressure points" of action that create problems. For example, some organizations go through regular "crunch times" when work demands become excessive. You know this if you have ever gone to a supermarket at 5:00 pm on a Friday afternoon. Crunch time happens every Friday afternoon in any large grocery store! Successful grocery managers prepare for and respond to the crunch.

Monitor the pressure points related to important performance factors in your organization. When do people and groups get geared up or worn down and why? Which groups systematically do better than others and how come? Where do consistent complaints or positive stories originate and what causes them? You can uncover problems and potential possibilities by exploring such patterns.

Watch the "flows" of how people interact to determine what supports or does not support desired results. Listen for any verbal cues that reveal organizational wide systemic challenges such as "don't speak up in meetings," "don't ask for help," and "just keep your head down and you won't get hurt."

Local level cues can also provide insight: "Don't bother asking that department, they never help," and, "Make sure he doesn't know about it because he will just make a fuss," indicate something worth attention.

Other types of patterns that deserve analysis include the ways new members are shown "the ropes" that must be learned in order to be accepted by the organization. For example, in some firms new recruits watch a film about the company and then an "experienced person" or "seasoned veteran" clarifies what is "real" and what part of the film was simply "public relations." This process can send a negative message or at least a mixed message about the organization that requires leadership direction.

Assess Assumptions: People (you and us included) do what they do based on assumptions. This is necessary to live your life. You assume the roads will be clear while driving to work on a sunny clear day. It would be impossible to check out all the variables that might impact your commute to work.

However, you might watch local TV or listen to the radio about the road conditions after a thunderous rainstorm or highly damaging winds to make sure that highways are clear. Test assumptions when certain pieces of information do not match. Ask others to explain what they know and why they believe it is valid to reveal their underlying assumptions. The inquiry about assumptions needs to be an honest exploration of the other's point of view.

Challenging others with a condescending tone rarely gains commitment. Uncover assumptions that you believe stand behind established practices. This provides insights into assumptions that may be out of date or at least limiting given current circumstances.

Assess Multiple Scenarios: Scenarios represent alternate courses of action based on different situational factors. Monitor situations in terms of a series of "if-then" alternatives. You can do so by yourself or with others.

For example, assume your organization has experienced a difficult and traumatic event (a layoff) or a potentially beneficial consequence (a new product launch). Chart out a best case, worst case, and most likely case scenario.

Assess the implications of each scenario. By analyzing all three you limit the chance that your understanding of the situation is based on "blue sky" beliefs (the best case). You also avoid getting stuck in the anxiety of failure (the worst case). But you risk the tendency to go for "half a loaf" by simply selecting a middle course between best and worst case — what most people choose (the most likely case).

Rely on Varied Monitoring Approaches: Vary your approach to avoid missing some aspect of the situation. Imagine using hours and hours of time to review industry publications and organization-wide documents. Your mind is consumed with the big picture. Break out of that approach for even a short period by focusing on a local issue that relates to some important more global factor.

For instance, take a walk on the shop floor and talk to a person dealing with a specific product or process. Or, after an extended period of time addressing specific questions, do the opposite and monitor the big picture.

Broaden your scope to think about how the details reflect upon the big picture. Going back and forth between big and local action can offer insights that might otherwise be missed. It also helps maintain flexibility in your thinking.

Vary your approach between task and process. Imagine being deeply engaged during a meeting in a discussion about accomplishing a specific task. Periodically lean back for a few minutes and put on your process awareness hat. Observe who interacts with whom, take note of how information gets processed, and pay attention to how decisions get made.

You can also vary your task and process analysis at the big picture level. After those hours reviewing the industry publications and organization-wide documents, take a walk through the plant and analyze the production process, noticing the flow of materials, people, and products. Review the strategic plan in terms of the process of its implementation versus the tasks it addresses.

Variance in how you approach situations expands your insights and understanding and maximizes your capacity to get the best sense of the situation possible.

Recognize that situational analysis is always the result of the meaning given to information and events. More important meanings can be revealed by monitoring and assessing patterns, assumptions, values, scenarios, and including a degree of variability in your approach. By using a variety of "How" approaches, you gain more useful interpretations. You also increase the possibility that you can verify what is going on and why.

Situational monitoring and assessment is perhaps the most difficult part of creating the Leadership Event because it is constant and never complete. Continuous analysis is the only way you can be sure you are reading things accurately. Situations change, sometimes dramatically. Yesterday's knowledge may not be relevant for today's challenges. What to do? Take former U.S. President Teddy Roosevelt's advice: "Do what you can, with what you have, where you are."

Put as much time, attention, and energy as you can into situational examination to gather as much valid and useful information as you can. Once your mind, heart, and gut recognize the need, take the lead and act! Be a "hungry," continuous learner and gather as much information as possible to maximize your success as a true leader!

Take Initiative

Recall that Leadership Events occur when the leader offers a direction and a first follower(s) supports it. The initiative of both generates the spark to create true leadership power.

The most useful initiatives have three important qualities:

- ✔ Appropriate — The initiative clearly matches important aspects of the situation and the current organizational culture and is perceived as doable with existing or attainable resources by potential followers

- ✔ Beneficial — The direction adds real value to individuals, groups, the organization, and customers

- ✔ Clearly Communicated — The initiative is understood and accepted by first followers so they multiply and generate enough momentum or "critical mass" to be carried out

Appropriate Initiatives

Appropriate initiatives match important aspects of the situation and can be accomplished. Imagine three situations in which you uncovered the "need to lead" based on your monitoring and assessing.

● *Situation 1:* An important customer's products are not being consistently delivered on time because the established delivery process does not take into account which customers are most prized by the organization. The customer complains and suggests cancelling future orders.

◆ *Initiative:* A change in the delivery scheduling process might resolve the problem and you are in charge of the scheduling process.

● *Situation 2:* A critical task force constantly gets bogged down because of poor communication skills among its members.

◆ *Initiative:* A short communication techniques training module or the assignment of a skilled facilitator could get the task force moving and you have an in-house trainer and facilitator available.

● *Situation 3:* A specific production facility develops an innovative way to improve product quality. No other facility produces the same product, but the quality enhancement could be applied to some products manufactured at other locations.

◆ *Initiative:* Send representatives from other plants to the location that created the quality enhancement and have them review how they could apply the process. Your boss has funds that can be budgeted for travel. You have a seat on a committee that oversees changes made in various plants.

Each of these initiatives matches an existing situational factor and can be accomplished based on current available resources.

Key questions to ask regarding an appropriate match between an initiative and the situation are:

✔ What could be done that would address the situation?

✔ What resources are needed?

✔ Who has control over those resources and can I gain their support?

Consider the Culture: The organization's culture must also be considered to determine the appropriateness of an initiative. Culture refers to the pattern of basic assumptions and set of shared beliefs that define an organization's "way of being" or "how we operate." Like the roots of a plant, culture represents the source from which people think, act, evaluate, respond, etc. within an organization or group.

Some organizations have very "strong" cultures which means the "way it is around here" is firmly entrenched in people's minds, hearts, and actions. People reinforce each other when they behave according to the culture standards and they confront those who stray from "our way."

Other organizations do not have such deeply defined ways of being. The standards for action and underlying values and beliefs are less clear and not as consistently communicated or invoked.

Some culture roots are beneficial to success while others limit organizational outcomes. For example, statements such as, "We deal with problems immediately," and, "We are always trying out different ways to improve," represent proactive culture roots that reflect getting positive results.

On the other hand, statements such as, "Do what you're told and no more," and, "Don't trust 'them,'" and, "That's not our problem," suggest defensive, negative culture roots that signal problems for an organization's success.

Shape and Mirror: Appropriate initiatives both "shape" and "mirror" the culture. Shaping initiatives create or mold the culture towards something better or different from what it is. They create or seek to modify action to realize more important and better outcomes. Shaping initiatives challenge people and groups to grow, improve, and adapt more effectively.

David Glass, who succeeded Sam Walton as Wal-Mart CEO shaped the company to achieve its mega-status as number one on the Fortune 500 list of companies. Glass instituted the use of technology to maximize the company's distribution and logistics operations. He launched the "superstore concept" and guided Wal-Mart's international expansion. As of 2006, the firm has 44 stores in China.

Shaping initiatives also bring out those staid business practices that no longer fit in a dynamic environment.

Shaping directions are appropriate when change must occur to survive and thrive in the situation. While CEO of Burger King in the 1980s, Barry Gibbons revived the "Have it your way" theme. He launched the highly successful broiled-chicken sandwich without the usual 18 months of market tests. Gibbons also set up a customer 800 number which receives thousands of calls per day and revitalized the customer responsiveness of the firm.

Appropriate initiatives must also mirror the existing aspects of the culture to be appropriate. A leader's direction will not be accepted if it is too far from the established culture roots. We can easily recognize the leader as a mirror in politics. Elected officials have always had to court the voters to win their approval. Today, more and more polls provide up to the minute feedback about the voters' needs and preferences. Elected officials must continually incorporate the latest input from their constituents.

The leader as shaper and mirror represents a challenge inherent in taking appropriate initiative. Leaders guide followers forward towards new and better results, but leader direction must also take followers where they want to go.

Appropriate initiatives stretch people beyond boundaries, and must be calibrated to mirror the path and speed at which people are willing to go. Effective leaders accept this contradictory aspect of taking initiative. They know that situations offer action opportunities to orchestrate events and they acknowledge the demands for a degree of fit with existing circumstances.

Beneficial Initiatives

People take action when they perceive value in the initiative. Beneficial directions offer individuals, groups, the organization, and customers something they want, need, and desire. Such initiatives resonate with the "WII-FM: What's In It For Me" reality that everyone experiences. All of us want some benefit from action. People do not take actions that they perceive as harmful, destructive, or non-life supporting to themselves.

Your monitoring and assessment actions should reveal issues that strike a chord with people's desires and their difficulties. Your direction must relate to these factors to gain momentum. The benefits may be immediate since they serve a very present need. Your direction may also provide long-term benefits. Your path may require some struggle at first in favor of value-added results down the road. Successful initiatives become action when their appropriateness and benefits get effectively communicated.

Clearly Communicated Initiatives

Clearly communicated leader initiatives create "shared meaning." Everyone understands this concept based on their experience.

Recall a time when you struggled to explain something to a person who just did not get what you were saying. You tried another way of getting your message across, and suddenly there was an "Ah, ha!" from the person. She or he exclaimed, "Oh, now I know what you mean!" With that comment, the connection called communication occurred.

Leader initiatives must create that commonality of understanding so that others accept the direction. The leader's initiative must make sense to the first follower for the Leadership Event to occur.

Nothing happens unless the first follower understands, agrees, and accepts your message. You may understand why an initiative is appropriate and provides meaningful benefits. Followers have to get the message before they agree.

Clearly communicated initiatives can multiply followers as they "get the meaning" and then generate enough momentum or "critical mass" so that the leader initiative is implemented and sustained.

Leadership Event initiatives get communicated in meetings (face-to-face, conference call, or on-line) when the leader speaks up and offers, suggests, proposes, and/or describes a course of action to others. The follower chimes in with a verbal agreement, affirmation, clarification or in some other way acknowledges support for the direction. Leadership initiatives can also take the form of a written document or email could also be the form takes.

The communication may be immediately obvious to others without much explanation beyond, "We should take this action." Typically, the message has to illustrate how the path of action is appropriate, adds value, and can be accomplished. That means initiatives must reflect the follower's WII-FM and be perceived by them as doable in the situation.

Communicate Details and General Themes: Communication that creates shared meaning involves many factors. Some of the more important factors relate to how people receive and interpret information. Each of us understands information in various "modes" or codes. One important and easily recognizable code is details or generalities.

Some people only get the message in terms of lots of details while others favor only a general overview.

Detail people like hundreds of specific facts and figures. They examine the fine print because every bit of information is important to them. In contrast, generalities people only emphasize "the bottom line" or big picture because that is all they find important.

Generality people like "the highlights" or an overview of main points because that gives them all they need to know. Generalities people review summary graphs and charts, and they make a quick cursory review of situations.

Each of us uses both details and generalities and we can go back and forth between them. Most people have a preference for one or the other. They become more comfortable with either details or generalities, which means initiatives must be communicated in terms of the follower's preferences.

Leaders can recognize detail and generality types based on their first responses to a spoken initiative. For example, consider the comments: "I need more information." "It would help me to know, specifically, how much will it cost." "Explain the background for your idea." These reflect the detail mode. Respond in kind with as much detail as necessary based on your situational analysis.

The first response from a generality person could be statements such as: "I want to know the bottom line." "Show me a summary chart of the plan." "Tell me the one thing that is most important." Be prepared to provide a short summary to communicate clearly for these requests.

Ask questions as you discuss your initiative to determine the detail and generality types. For instance, you could ask questions such as: "What else do you need to know?" "Do you have enough information?" "What more can I tell you?" Detail people will reply, "Well, I'll have to go over all the numbers, and get some background reports." A generality person will retort, "I only need to see the total cost," or, "Just go over the big picture again."

When your initiative is communicated in writing, you can recognize detail people because they carefully review almost all of the material you give them. They point out multiple items that raise issues for them even those that may seem obscure.

A document returned from a detail person will be well handled (many folded pages, lots of dog eared corners, notes in the margins, and generally worn looking paper). Have a well prepared set of detailed specifics to satisfy such individuals.

Generality people read the document's overview or simply flip through the pages seeking to "get the gist of it." They may highlight just one or two items. A document read by a general person will remain in pristine shape (few creases, no marks, only one or two pages handled). Include an executive summary as the first page for a written initiative to write clearly for such people.

Use Statistics and Stories: Statistics and stories provide another important way to clearly communicate initiatives and create shared meaning. These tools ramp up your message. They are communication instruments that can convey compelling clarity and resonate with different aspects of people's information processing.

Statistics influence the rational, left brain. Stories speak to one's "soft side" that is touched less by a figure or fact. Stories impact the right brain and represent an age old communication method. Their power stems from how they represent a complex idea or capture an important idea in a vivid example. Statistics and stories combine to create a potent message.

Add choice statistics to enhance communication clarity. Quantify your direction with accurate data. Select valid, qualified evidence to support your view. Rely on your own experience bank of key events and meaningful moments for anecdotes.

Read business magazines and books for additional stories. Keep a catalogue of such stories as a reference tool. Ask others to tell you their stories to gather additional examples.

Create Two Way Communication: Obviously, clear communication (from the root words "community" and "commonality") also results with a dialogue. Two way communication maximizes understanding and acceptance.

Four important techniques maximize dialogue clarity.

✔ Seek information to create more dialogue. Imagine you have offered a direction in a meeting. A person in the meeting voices some misgivings about taking the action now because of other factors in your organization's environment. Rather than give more information about why your initiative is appropriate and beneficial, seek information from the person to get a dialogue going. Make statements such as: _"Tell me more." "What else?" "What makes you say that?"_ or simply be silent to prompt others to keep talking. Seeking information gets and keeps people talking with you about your initiative.

✔ Restate information from others to demonstrate your desire for dialogue. Restate a key word or phrase the person said with an affirmative tone. Consider this statement in response to an initiative: *"We don't have the resources."* A simple restatement, *"You think we can't get the resources,"* affirms that you heard the person and typically causes the person to say, *"That's right,"* which sets the stage for more dialogue since they moved from disagreement to agreement with you. Restating facilitates dialogue whereas disagreement generates distance.

✔ Probe for deeper meanings and alternate issues. Probing allows you to get behind initial concerns to reveal more substantive reactions to your initiative. Suppose someone challenged your initiative because they felt it would create too much work for already overburdened staff. A useful probe could be, *"I understand the work load is heavy. How do you perceive this action increasing the load?"* or, *"The staff is stretched thin. How will our current approach help them compared to the changes offered in my idea?"*

Such questions enable you to better understand the core reasons for resistance to your initiative. That information can support a dialogue in which you can discuss the necessary additional items to gain the person's support.

✔ Summarize to clarify your understanding of what people said (content) and the underlying intent (feeling) behind their comments. To illustrate, in relation to the example comments above, you could summarize by saying: *"You are concerned about resources,"* (content summary). *"And, it sounds like you and others are overwhelmed with work now,"* (feeling summary).

An effective summary causes the other person to say, *"Yes, that is exactly right."* Such responses create a desire for additional dialogue which gives you the chance to continue to explain the appropriateness and benefits behind your initiative.

Timing Your Message is Everything: Timing your communication of initiative is essential. Sometimes it is necessary and appropriate to test a proposed direction. The notion that leaders get it right the first time is only true in fictional stories or the movies.

Testing a direction provides a chance to verify how well you have monitored and assessed the situation. It also allows you to determine the degree to which your direction matches the established organizational culture roots.

Send up "trial balloons" to determine how the initiative flies. You can ask others for an opinion about an idea without indicating it is a preferred course of action. First followers can also test a direction by responding with, *"The idea sounds good to me. Let's consider it some more. What do you think?"*

In some circumstances, it is more skillful for the leader to float a direction with established allies first. Allies typically assume a collaborative posture as opposed to discounting a direction. Allies are more likely to make the time to think through issues related to the initiative rather than deflect it because they are "too busy now for this stuff." They are more likely to help leaders work through how their direction relates to situational factors rather than point out its flaws.

First Followers can also benefit by relying on their confirmed allies by asking, "What do you think?" before they fully commit to a course of action.

Obviously, the sense of urgency or immediacy must always come into play when offering an initiative. "He who hesitates is lost." Some situations require bulling ahead because they are critical and demand immediate action. Other circumstances allow additional time to consider, rethink, and evaluate actions.

Pick your spots when you take initiative. Key players whose support is necessary may need to be present before offering a course of action. An initiative that requires top management approval is one example. There may be no value in charting a course without the CEO present if she/he must commit to it before others even consider the idea.

Working behind the scenes and informally talking about your initiative with a variety of key players can often assure success prior to the actual presentation in a formal meeting.

No Initiative is Ever Perfect

Some will never follow an initiative. Perhaps others cannot see how the direction appropriately matches the situation no matter what you say. Some may not believe the benefits are worth the effort given their values and interests. Maybe the initiative was not or could not be communicated clearly given time constraints. Bad timing also kills many initiatives.

These difficulties might be overcome with more effort, greater persistence, and more skill on the leader's part. And, even then, some will never accept an initiative no matter what. The fact that some will never follow cannot be ignored. Leaders can minimize such situations. They can establish the important foundational support for their initiatives by building quality relationships with key individuals, based on trust, care, and mutual respect.

Establish the Necessary Ground Work

Leadership Events emerge from a power of partnership that cannot be coerced. Leaders and followers have to *want* to join together in action to respond to situational factors. That means the "W Factor" — the will to act — must be lively in the awareness of both.

The potential to create Leadership Events increases when the necessary ground work to gain commitment is firmly laid and continuously reinforced. The ground work forms the foundational footing necessary to get people to want to listen and support you.

The ground work factors are, borrowing from Will Rogers, "Common sense that ain't so common." Most people know about the ground work; but knowing is not doing, and doing does not mean we do it well.

Three essential actions contribute to forming the necessary ground work to create Leadership Events:

- ✔ Create common ground
- ✔ Build trust
- ✔ Build and reinforce your "credibility rating"

Create Common Ground

Common ground unites people. We feel more comfortable and open when we share something in common with another.

A commonality between leaders and followers enables them to support each other to create Leadership Events. They agree about what must be done to address situational factors. They experience a bond based upon established principles, expectations, beliefs, and values. They sense an identity with each other as people and participants within their organization.

Seek ways to establish and reinforce common ground whenever the opportunity arises. For example, clarify your sense of a situation as you monitor and assess it to identify common points of agreement with potential followers. Explore underlying assumptions as a way to find the deeper sense of unity that could bind others to you. For example, consider a situation where someone disagrees with you about a specific direction. By examining the person's underlying assumption, you might find some agreement at a more subtle level of interpretation. Work from that level to achieve a commonality of purpose.

Make connections with others in terms of their background, values, interests, and goals. With some people you can discuss both professional and personal issues. Others will feel more comfortable maintaining their personal privacy so seek commonality about work related issues.

Meet people at their level and work with them at their pace. For example, ask, "What do you like about your job?" What got you interested in this type of work?" Where do you hope to be professionally in the next five years?" Respond with information about yourself that illustrates a similarity that is meaningful to you and should resonate with the other's experience.

Clarify your expectations and ask others about their expectations as a way to find common places of accord. Expectations could relate to work in general, the organization's mission, vision, and values, or a specific task. Listen for expectations that others offer and point out where you share their view.

Common ground building is on-going. It may be too late to seek commonality once you are in a fray trying to create a

Leadership Event. Work on common ground building every day. It also makes the work place more pleasant when you and others operate from a shared identity.

Build Trust

Trust is the super glue that binds people together in a seamless partnership of mutual respect, shared sense of values, and willingness to be open with each other. Trust is contagious. Trust begets trust. With trust, people encourage each other, are more willing to be involved, and feel confident in each other. This creates the willingness to take initiative and offer greater allegiance.

Distrust divides people. We do not give unqualified trust to someone who is not and cannot be a part of us. People follow those they trust and do not follow those they distrust. Leaders offer direction because they trust that others will support them. No one initiates action if they believe it will be automatically shot down.

Every interaction with others is a "moment of trust." Every behavior either develops or destroys some aspect of trust between people. Continuous attention to trust building is essential. Common ground building facilitates trust building since we trust those with whom we can identify. Trust remains limited with little or no commonality since that separation fosters suspicion and doubt.

Trust building results from a variety of actions including:

✔ Do what you say. Consistency creates trust.

✔ Make a promise and keep it. Do not make promises you cannot keep.

✔ Take in a confidence and vow to absolutely never betray it. Do not gossip.

✔ Accept responsibility for your actions and results. Do not make excuses.

✔ Be more open with information. Avoid secrecy which says, "I do not trust you."

✔ Extend your trust of others a little further. Being trusted creates trust.

✔ Tell the truth; the truth builds trust...and it is always easier to remember the truth.

Trust building takes time and effort. Allot the time and take the action necessary. You cannot build a tall building on a skimpy foundation.

Build and Reinforce Credibility

Credibility means believability. A person's "credibility rating" reflects the extent to which others believe in the person and the person's ideas.

Those you need as followers rate your credibility based on their sense about you. And, others respond to you when you are the first follower based on how they rate you in that role.

High credibility equates to people perceiving you as dependable, reliable, and worthy of their support. Political polls basically represent credibility tests about how the voters perceive the candidates. Such polls are done periodically.

Your credibility gets rated every day by others based on what you say and do or do not say or do. The higher your rating, just like the higher a politician's poll numbers, the more likely people will support your initiatives.

Credibility can be likened to the leader's DNA since it reflects the entire coding structure of a relationship. The degree of common ground and level of trust get summed up in terms of credibility perceptions. That means common ground creating efforts and trust building enhance your credibility rating.

You can also increase your credibility rating when you:

✔ Identify the credibility factors. Ask people what they feel indicates credibility. Have them define the specific behaviors that demonstrate credibility. If necessary, ask them to rank order the factors in terms of which are most important to them.

✔ Demonstrate your capacity. Take action to illustrate your credibility based on the factors identified. For example, assume people tell you that work related expertise matters. Actively enhance and demonstrate your expertise. If credibility means helping others, seek ways to do so. Demonstrating credibility does not mean being underhanded or manipulative. Your intentions determine the purpose of your behavior. You have control over your intentions. Your intention here needs to reveal that you are a credible person in terms that others recognize as valid.

✔ Admit mistakes when it is justified. Integrity increases credibility. Cover-ups, fraud, and underhanded dealings create cynicism. Admitting honest mistakes builds credibility. It distinguishes you from the unsavory lot who try to conceal their mistakes.

Recognize that credibility building is an on-going process. You can make a big success and boost your credibility rating over night. You can also blunder and plummet your rating to zero. Like common ground and trust, credibility ground work needs to be laid on a continuous basis.

The Limits Leaders Always Face

You face a variety of constraints when you try to take the lead. You may not be able to use the necessary time to establish ground work. Your skill level may not be adequate at this stage to apply effective ground work building. There may not be enough ground available for the necessary foundation to get some people to follow. Some will never feel a sense of unity and trust towards you or perceive you as credible.

These very real limits mean you may not be able to gain the necessary first follower or create the required critical mass to generate a Leadership Event. Adversity is not an adequate deterrent. It is the duty of the leaders to lead, of the creative to create, and of the daring to do.

Think about your "W Factor" the next time you feel the dismay and exhaustion of failing to gain followers. Review your reasons for making attempts to create Leadership Events. Ideally you want to fulfill your organization's purpose, serve a customer, right some injustice, and make a meaningful difference. These are noble and necessary pursuits. They deserve another infusion of energy despite the difficulties their pursuit creates.

Reinforce Leadership Events

Your success creating Leadership Events depends partly on the larger framework within which you operate.

You may create a set of Leadership Events based on your on-going and unwavering will and your highly refined individual skill. However, your long-term impact requires that *others* also emerge to create their own bursts of true leadership power.

A "leadership culture" must exist.

That means an important and ever present belief, value, assumption throughout the organization must be that Leadership Events matter. The culture must recognize and reinforce the actions of taking the lead and stepping up as a first follower.

The underlying principles here are:

✔ What gets rewarded gets continued, and

✔ Everyone enjoys being sincerely appreciated for actions they believe are important.

You can be a prime player by using these principles to usher in and/or push the organization further forward towards forming a leadership culture. An important step towards this end is to remember again the important role both leaders and first followers play in creating Leadership Events.

We typically reward only the leaders. Following is viewed as a second-class activity. Yet, no one wants to be second class. Acknowledging only leaders means we inadvertently limit the power of true leadership. If only the leader role matters, no one will want to follow so no would- be leaders ever gain support.

Tune in to MMFG-AM

A simple and profound action you can take immediately is to Tune in to MMFG-AM — appreciate those who create Leadership Events. MMFG-AM stands for Make Me Feel Good About Myself.

Everyone wants to be recognized and appreciated. Everyone experiences a boost when given even a simple acknowledgment such as, "You did a good job today."

Give people a word of praise after they take the lead or step up as first followers. A simple statement, "You got the group going on the ABC project," tells the leader you value her effort. A short comment, "When you spoke up to support Mary Ann, the entire group supported the effort," clarifies your admiration for a first follower.

Praise in Public: Acknowledge people's contribution to Leadership Events in public settings. Take the powerful example of Ron Victor, Superintendent of the Garfield Heights School District. Victor's career passion consistently guides him to make substantial improvements in the quality of education. To further his efforts, Ron convinced the city Mayor, Tom Longo, to join him in creating "Leadership Garfield Heights."

This initiative sought to involve all sectors of the community in a series of large and small group meetings to address the issue of how everyone could and needed to play a role to improve the schools.

Victor's first step involved organizing a two-day retreat to be attended by school principles, school board members, City

Council members, heads of all the major churches, local business owners and senior executives, parents, and students. Over 100 people attended the program. The group discussed how everyone could participate as leaders and followers. They generated key areas that needed attention. They developed action teams to address each area.

Ron Victor orchestrated two more large group sessions and multiple small group meetings over the next 18 months as the effort evolved. The substantial progress created by this initiative generated a positive stir from other school districts. As a result, Victor and the Mayor were asked to make a series of presentations about Leadership Garfield Heights across the state and at professional conferences.

Ron Victor deserves substantial credit for Leadership Garfield Heights. Yet, because he is a highly conscious person, he spent considerable time giving recognition to others for their contributions to the process.

He consistently acknowledged the roles others played in public settings. His public recognition fueled additional interest in the project.

Alter the Reward System: A long-term strategy to reinforce Leadership Events involves working to change the formal organizational reward system. True leadership cultures exist when the formal performance management system includes an emphasis on both leader and first follower behaviors.

Get started today and have a three to five year time frame in mind. Consider who you could talk with immediately to generate discussion about the factors included in the performance management system. Expand the effort by involving others to create a core cadre of the committed around the idea. Armed with a strong support group, "lead up" by going to the next level of management with the intent to involve them in thinking through the situation.

Recognize that systemic change takes time and often requires taking a step or two backwards and/or making some detours to get to your ultimate destination. Keep your mind on the goal and ignore getting stuck in the obstacles. The legacy you leave will enable people to fulfill the organization and themselves.

Block Negative Leadership Events

Assume you consistently do the work of true leadership. You monitor and assess, take initiative, establish the groundwork, and reinforce others who create Leadership Events. In some situations you may have to take the opposite track.

Instead of leading towards something, it may be necessary to use a blocking maneuver to stop another person's negative leadership direction. That is, you might need to counter rather than reinforce another's Leadership Event.

The necessity for such action stems from an important leadership reality:

Just because someone leads and others follow
does not mean their actions increase productivity,
create more justice, enhance the greater good,
increase the positive elements, or generate
life-supporting effects.

Leaders at the both "big" and local level can create havoc and harm. Think of the many well known examples of leaders who gained massive numbers of followers and ultimately deceived, lied, or in other ways served only narrow, divisive, and destructive interests. Adolph Hitler. Reverend Jim Jones. Jeff Skilling, former head of Enron. Bernie Ebbers, former head of World Com, and the heads of hate groups like the KKK.

Think of your own experience. Have you ever observed any of these negative examples of leadership:

- ✔ An individual gets a small clique to constantly criticize and complain about everything. The clique's comments create destructive conflict and destroys overall morale.

- ✔ A person in a unit or division gains support from members to use power plays and garner resources only for that group. Other units suffer as a result of such manipulative actions.

- ✔ People support someone who tries to cover-up problems, blame others, or refuses to take responsibility for their actions.

It is interesting that such leaders and followers can and do emerge. Consider the reality that no organization's vision, mission, and value statements include phrases such as:

"Make harsh comments about others," or,

"Criticize anyone who does not agree with you," or,

"Don't be a team player," or,

"Do what ever it takes to get what you want and don't care about anyone else," or,

"Lie, cheat, and deceive just don't get caught," or,

"We only promote employees who suck up to the boss and undermine fellow employees."

Yet, "negative" leaders—those who do not support the organization's purpose—emerge.

The fact that you want to create Leadership Events that provide positive benefit is to your credit, a function of your personal state of awareness—your "W Factor." Others lead and follow based on their consciousness and what they want. You need to step up in the face of negative, destructive, harmful leadership efforts.

You must have the courage to block negative leadership actions so that you can also fulfill your organization's purpose by creating a critical mass of moments that move towards the desired ends.

A starting place is to simply point out the results and consequences of an initiative. Make a statement that reveals the outcomes such as, "This suggestion will provide one division with all the resources we have available." Then clarify the negative impact of the action, "By only serving that one division, morale and success in other divisions will be hurt."

Challenge a direction in terms of how it matches the group or organization's goals. Remind people of the important goals and then inquire how the direction impacts their achievement. Engage others to offer their interpretation of a negative Leadership Event. Call upon those who should be able to clarify the ineffective impact of such events.

It may be necessary to make your stand in a public setting such as a group meeting. Recall the image of the young Chinese man who stood in front of the tanks at Tiananmen

Square in 1989. You may have to muster a similar level of courage and step up in an overt and highly visible manner.

You can also talk to people individually and in small groups and gain their support to block a negative leadership action. You can gain the necessary backup support you need to publically challenge a negative leadership direction when you have an established group already behind you.

You increase your chances of success by continually establishing new relationships and reinforcing existing ones. It is a never ending effort!

The willingness to counter other's leadership always involves risk. Only you can decide whether the risk is worth the effort. Only you can work on yourself so you take reasonable risks. You have to look within yourself to address these issues.

Here are four simple decision rules to consider as you make your choice:

✔ Will it take more effort and energy to face up to the harmful leadership initiative now, or will it be more difficult later after the initiative gains substantial momentum?

✔ If you do not take action, who will? When? With what impact?

✔ What is the worst thing that will happen to you if you do take countering action?

✔ Is someone else either positioned or more skilled to counter the negative action so that you can proactively support their efforts as a first follower?

We believe your responses will bring out the best of what you are. We operate based on the precept that you want to create more positive results for everyone and that you will demonstrate the courage to block negative leadership action.

Your Leadership Event Action Plan

Recall the questions in the first two paragraphs on the first page of this book:

✔ Have you ever been in a meeting and suggested a way to solve a problem and the entire group agreed with you and was motivated to carry out your course of action?

✔ Can you recall a time when a team member proposed an action that you thought would be very useful so you spoke up to support it? As a result, the entire team joined in and adopted the path of action.

Your "Yes!" response indicates you have created Leadership Events in the past. By reading this far, you are now armed with the knowledge and insights necessary to create additional Leadership Events in a more skillful and consistent manner. It is time to take action in a planned and purposeful way to maximize your skillful implementation!

A good starting point involves a review of the actions provided throughout this book and your current capacity to perform each.

Complete the "Action List Review and Skill Assessment" table below. Then complete the "Leadership Event Skill Development Plan" to determine what you want to work on and how to get started.

Action List Review and Skill Assessment

Review the 90 actions on the following chart. They represent the key suggestions to apply the content of this book. Assess your current skill level in the column to the right of each statement using the following scale:

1	2	3	4	5
Very Low	Low	Average	High	Very High

Consider asking others whom you trust to assess you also. They may give you insights into how you apply the skills versus how you think you apply them.

Action List   *Current Skill Level*

Your "W Factor"	
1. I take the necessary initiative to contribute to creating Leadership Events.	
2. I create Leadership Events that support the organization's primary purpose (vision, mission, values) and serve its customers (both external and internal).	
3. I consistently recognize and reinforce others who manifest Leadership Events.	
4. I counter individuals who offer direction and gain support for actions that do not serve an organization's vision, mission, and values.	
5. I work continuously on myself based on a formal action plan to improve my true leadership skills.	

Action List   *Current Skill Level*

Monitor and Assess Situations	
1. I monitor and assess other important players in our business/market.	
2. I monitor and assess new technological developments that could impact our business.	
3. I monitor and assess social-political trends that could affect the organization.	
4. I monitor and assess the match between the organization's current vision, mission and values and our environment	

5. I monitor and assess organization-wide issues related to policy, finance, production, marketing, and human resources areas.	
6. I monitor and assess how current organizational systems effect the total enterprise.	
7. I monitor and assess the needs, wants, and interests of important customers.	
8. I monitor and assess important product quality factors and how they are created, refined, and received.	
9. I monitor and assess the impact of policy, finance, production, marketing, and human resources functions at the local level.	
10. I monitor and assess specific goals and what they indicate for success at the local level.	
11. I monitor and assess outcomes and results based on how people interact at meetings.	
12. I recognize situations in meetings that require my heightened focus of attention.	
13. I observe both task and process challenges during regularly scheduled "formal" meetings	
14. I compare a meeting's defined purpose with key issues the group faces.	
15. I watch for signals that indicate stumbling blocks for individuals and groups.	
16. I pay attention to signs that suggest ways to solve problems.	

17. I listen for opportunities that could be beneficial.	
18. I pro-actively survey information related to my job requirements.	
19. I seek information and insights that suggest a gap between what is and what could be.	
20. I seek ways to add real value and make a meaningful difference	
21. I observe patterns that create problems.	
22. I watch how people interact to determine what supports or does not support desired results.	
23. I listen for verbal cues that reveal organizational wide systemic challenges.	
24. I analyze the ways new members are shown "the ropes" during their orientation to the organization.	
25. I clarify assumptions and then test them to understand how well they match other information.	
26. I listen for values messages that reveal important ways people judge what is good or bad, right or wrong, important or unimportant.	
27. I suggest scenarios (alternate responses to specific situations) to determine courses of action.	
28. I analyze situations from the big picture and detailed level and in terms of task and process.	

Action List   *Current Skill Level*

Take Initiative	
1. I consider what could be done that would address situations that need improvement.	
2. I determine the resources that are needed for an initiative.	
3. I find out who has control over needed resources and seek their support.	
4. I consider how well an initiative matches the organization's critical culture roots.	
5. I "shape" the culture to move it towards something better or different from what it is.	
6. I "mirror" the culture and reinforce some of its important existing aspects.	
7. I identify the specific WII-FM's for key followers.	
8. I know the benefits an initiative provides for critical followers.	
9. I create 'shared meaning" so followers understand my initiative.	
10. I know which followers prefer detailed information and which prefer general information.	
11. I use details and general information when necessary.	

12. I use appropriate statistics to explain my initiative.	
13. I use appropriate stories to communicate and create shared meaning.	
14. I engage others in a dialogue of two way communication.	
15. I seek information to create more dialogue.	
16. I restate information from others to demonstrate my desire for dialogue.	
17. I probe for deeper meanings and alternate issues.	
18. I summarize what people say (content) and the underlying intent (feeling) behind their comments.	
19. I time my communication to maximize clarity and understanding.	
20. I send up "trial balloons" to determine how an initiative will be received.	
21. I rely on established allies to test out initiatives.	
22. I recognize the need for urgency of action.	
23. I accept that some will never follow my initiatives and continue to seek followers for initiatives that are truly important.	

Action List   *Current Skill Level*

Establish the Necessary Ground Work	
1. I create common ground.	
2. I compare my sense of a situation with others to identify points of agreement.	
3. I explore underlying assumptions to find deeper levels of commonality.	
4. I connect with others in terms of their personal and/or professional) background, interests, and goals.	
5. I clarify my expectations regarding any aspects of work.	

Action List   *Current Skill Level*

Build trust	
1. I do what I say I will do.	
2. When I make promises, I keep them.	
3. I never betray confidences.	
4. I accept responsibility for my actions and results and do not make excuses.	
5. I am open with information and avoid secrecy.	
6. I extend my trust of others a little further.	
7. I always tell the truth	
8. I make the time to build trust.	

Action List   *Current Skill Level*

Build and Reinforce Credibility	
1. I identify the credibility factors others use.	
2. I demonstrate my capacity in key credibility areas.	
3. I admit mistakes when it is justified.	

Action List   *Current Skill Level*

Reinforce the Leadership Events	
1. I apply the principle: what gets rewarded gets continued.	
2. I apply the principle: everyone enjoys being sincerely appreciated for actions they believe are important.	
3. I recognize leaders and first followers.	
4. I appreciate others (tune in to MMFG-AM) with sincere recognition for action and results.	
5. I acknowledge people's contribution in public settings when appropriate.	
6. I lead up to include rewarding leaders and followers in the formal organizational reward system.	

Action List   *Current Skill Level*

Reinforce the Leadership Events	
1. I use blocking maneuvers to stop a negative Leadership Event.	
2. I point out the results or consequences of what I perceive as a negative initiative.	
3. I describe how an initiative creates a negative impact.	
4. I challenge initiatives in terms of how they match the group or organization's goals.	
5. I remind people of the important goals and then inquire how the direction impacts their achievement.	
6. I engage others to offer their interpretation of negative Leadership Events.	
7. I call upon those who should be able to clarify the ineffective impact of negative Leadership Events.	
8. I ask myself, will it take more effort and energy to face up in the moment and counter a harmful leadership initiative, or will it be more difficult later after the initiative gains substantial momentum?	
9. I ask myself, if I do not take action, who will? When? With what impact?	
10. I ask myself, what is the worst thing that will happen to me if I do take countering action?	

Leadership Event Skill Development Plan

Now that you have a sense of your current skill level, identify a specific approach to improve your skills in areas that are most important to you or your organization. Include a time frame for your plan. See the sample Leadership Skill Development Plan on page 98. Use additional paper if necessary to create your action plans. Solicit support from others by asking them to be your coaching partners to complete your plan. They can help you stay on track and you can reciprocate by supporting them.

Sample Development Plan

This development plan focuses on one key "Take Initiative" action. Note specific steps identify benefits, explore deeper benefits if necessary, and how to communicate the benefits in terms of the specific initiative.

The Completion Dates identify a reasonable time frame for each action.

Leadership Skill Development Plan - **Sample**

Skill

> Take Initiative #7 - I identify the specific "What's In It
> For Me" (WII-FM) for key followers.

Approach (list specific steps)	*Completion Date*
1. List key followers needed for initiative "X"	April 23
2. Meet with each person to discuss benefits they value.	April 29
3. Summarize on paper the important benefits of each person.	April 30
4. Analyze the current initiative to determine where it does and does not provide desired benefits.	April 30
5. If necessary, revisit with specific followers to explore alternate benefits.	May 1-2
6. Outline specific points to present that demonstrate where the initiative matches benefits.	May 2

Coaching Partners

Susan Williams
Jonathan Billingsworth

Leadership Event Skill Development Plan

Skill

Approach (list specific steps)	*Completion Date*

Coaching Partners

Concluding Note from the Authors

Congratulations on reading our book and creating your Leadership Event Skill Development Plan.

We invite you to continue your development and expand the quality of leadership throughout your organization. The Leadership Group and LEADS organizations offer training seminars, consulting workshops, and speaking services to organizations to create a leadership culture.

Contact us at:

Warren Blank
The Leadership Group
505 Beachland Boulevard
Suite 223
Vero Beach, Florida 32963
919-656-3344
LeaderWB@aol.com

Aaron Brown
LEAD Associates
P.O. Box 371316
Denver, Colorado 80237
303-718-1358
LEADASSOCIATES1@aol.com

About the Authors

Warren Blank is President of The Leadership Group, a firm formed in 1986 with offices in Vero Beach, FL and Chapel Hill, NC. The Leadership Group clients include over 50 Fortune 500 firms and more than 80 different government agencies. Warren has a Ph.D. and MBA from the University of Cincinnati, an M.S. in Education from Indiana
University and a B.A. from the University of Akron. He is the author of *The 108 Skills of Natural Born Leaders* (AMACOM 2001), *The Nine Natural Laws of Leadership - 2nd Edition* (Leadership Group 2006), and *Leadership Skills for Managers* (American Management Institute 1995), and many articles in professional journals. Find out more at LeadershipGroup.com.

Aaron Brown, based in Denver, Colorado, is President of LEAD Associates which provides Leadership Education, Assessment and Development services to individuals and organizations. Aaron has over thirty years of progressive management experience both in the public and private sectors. He has successfully designed and delivered
hundreds of leadership training programs to over 20,000 participants. He is co-author of *The Nine Natural Laws of Leadership* and the forth coming book, *People Won't Follow Leaders They Don't Like*.

Order additional copies of

*The Leadership Event: The Moments of True
Leadership that Move Organizations*

2nd Edition - January 2006

Contact:
The Leadership Group 919-656-3344
LeaderWB@aol.com

Quantity discounts are available